My name is

_____

I am_____years old

I love my **Mango** Book

Copyright © DC Books
First Published July 2009

Printed in India
DC Press Pvt. Ltd., Kochi

Publisher
DC Books
387,1st Cross, 4th Block, 80 ft Peripheral Road, Koramangala, Bangalore 560 034, Karnataka, India
D C Kizhakemuri Edam, Good Shepherd Street, Kottayam 686 001, Kerala, India
Website: www.mangobooks.net
Email: editorial@mangobooks.net

No portion of this book may be reproduced
or transmitted in any form or by any means
without the prior written permission of the publisher.
All rights reserved.
ISBN 978-81-264-2403-0
MANGO M0060

DC Books: The first Indian Book Publishing House to get ISO Certification

RAMA STORIES

THE STORY OF JATAYU

RETOLD BY **APARNA NAMBIAR**
ILLUSTRATED BY **V S MADHU**

THE SETTING

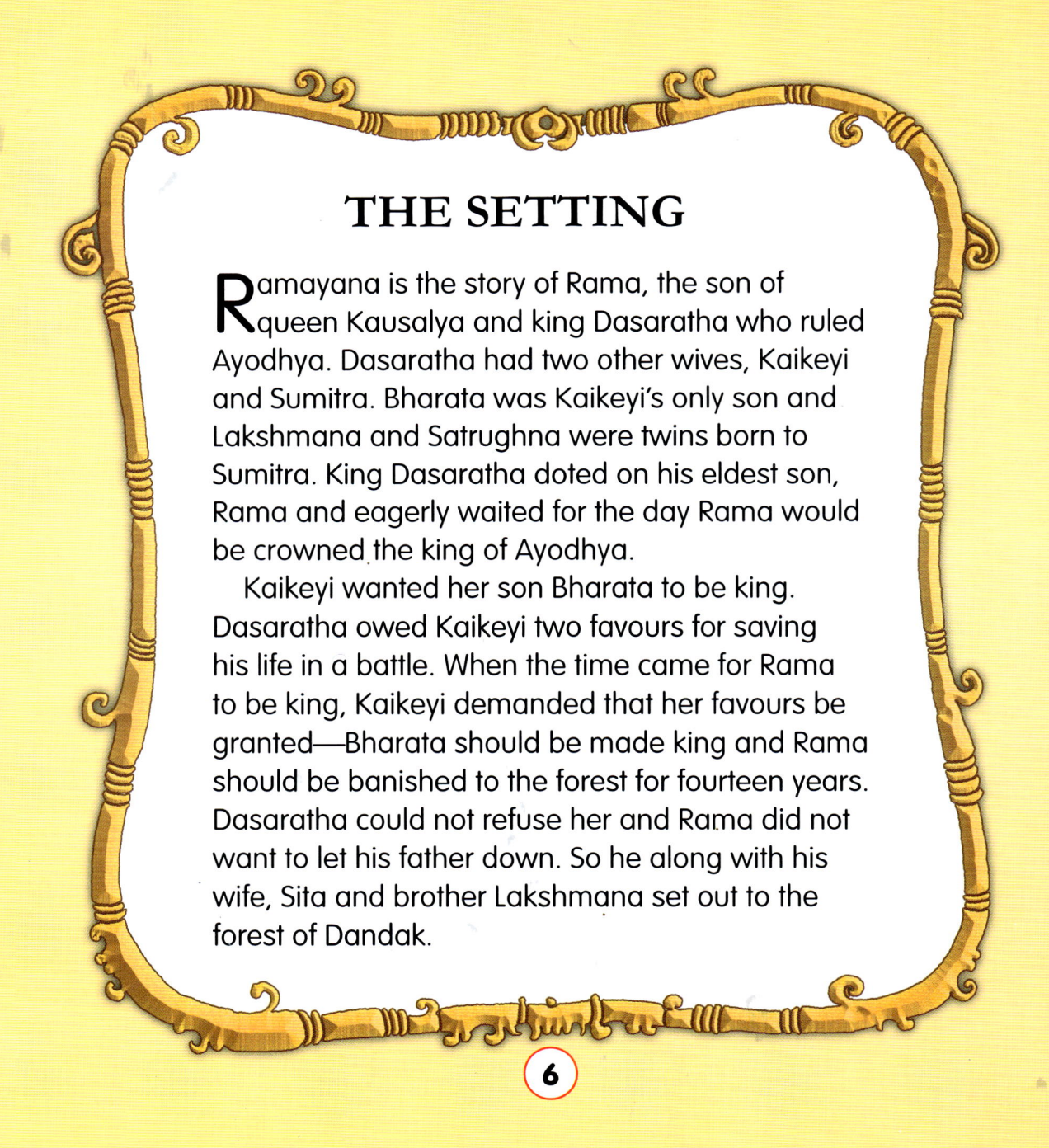

Ramayana is the story of Rama, the son of queen Kausalya and king Dasaratha who ruled Ayodhya. Dasaratha had two other wives, Kaikeyi and Sumitra. Bharata was Kaikeyi's only son and Lakshmana and Satrughna were twins born to Sumitra. King Dasaratha doted on his eldest son, Rama and eagerly waited for the day Rama would be crowned the king of Ayodhya.

Kaikeyi wanted her son Bharata to be king. Dasaratha owed Kaikeyi two favours for saving his life in a battle. When the time came for Rama to be king, Kaikeyi demanded that her favours be granted—Bharata should be made king and Rama should be banished to the forest for fourteen years. Dasaratha could not refuse her and Rama did not want to let his father down. So he along with his wife, Sita and brother Lakshmana set out to the forest of Dandak.

This is the story of Jatayu the chivalrous vulture—a true friend to King Dasaratha and an ardent devotee of Lord Rama. Jatayu and his brother Sampati heard of the arrival of Rama, Sita and Lakshmana in the Dandak forest and they rushed to greet them. Jatayu and Sampati offered to help them during their exile.

Years passed. Jatayu grew old. One day, as he was resting on a tree, he heard a woman's cries for help. He looked around. Flying in the air was Ravana in his chariot, the Pushpaka Vimana and with him was a beautiful woman crying pitifully.

Jatayu took a closer look and recognised Sita. Ravana was carrying Sita away! Jatayu could not let this happen.

He had grown old and he knew he was no match for the mighty Ravana. Yet he was not afraid. "I have to save Sita at any cost," he thought.

He spread out his huge wings and flew towards Ravana's chariot, chanting the name of Rama. "Let go of Sita or I shall kill you!" he cried. Ravana ignored his threat. "What can a silly bird do to me?" he thought. Jatayu's powerful wings lashed out at Ravana. He tore off one of the railing bars of the chariot.

"Help me, Jatayu!" cried Sita. Jatayu gently picked Sita up from the chariot and placed her on the ground. He then lashed out at Ravana again, digging his sharp claws into Ravana's flesh. He began to strike at his heads and arms but they miraculously grew back in place. Jatayu soon began to feel tired from the fight.

Ravana sensed that Jatayu was beginning to feel worn out. He pulled out his sword and fought back. But Jatayu did not give up. He attacked Ravana over and over again. The fight continued for a long time.

Soon, Jatayu was severely wounded and could fight no more. Ravana took advantage of this and with one strong swing, cut off one of Jatayu's wings. Jatayu fell to the ground crying, "Rama! Rama!"

Jatayu was in pain, as he lay bleeding. Sita ran up to him and embracing him said, "You have sacrificed your life to save me." She could not bear to see him suffer. But at that very moment, Ravana swooped down and grabbed Sita. He pulled her back into the chariot and resumed his journey back to Lanka.

Jatayu knew he did not have much time left. Before he died he wanted to tell Rama about Sita's abduction. He kept uttering Rama's name to keep his spirits up. His voice grew faint but he knew he had to stay alive.

Jatayu did not have too wait long. Soon Rama and Lakshmana came running towards him. Rama sat down beside Jatayu and took him in his arms, "Who did this to you, Jatayu?" he asked.

"Ravana has abducted Sita," Jatayu whispered. "I tried to stop him but he was too strong for me. He has fled south. Go after him and rescue Sita." Saying this, Jatayu breathed his last in Rama's arms.

Rama and Lakshmana were heart-broken at the loss of a great friend. Rama asked Lakshmana to make a funeral pyre for Jatayu. Together, they carried Jatayu's body to the pyre and performed his last rites. Burdened with grief at the death of their friend Jatayu, Rama and Lakshmana continued their journey south in search of Sita.

When they met Sampati, Jatayu's brother, Rama told him in a grave voice, "Brave Jatayu is no more. He lost his life trying to save Sita from the clutches of Ravana."

A grief-stricken Sampati said to Rama, "Rama, you must continue your search for Sita and avenge my brother's death. I am too old now to fight Ravana. He lives in Lanka on the far side of the ocean. You have to cross it to get there."

Rama and Lakshmana thanked Sampati. They then set out towards Mahendra Hill from where they would cross over to Lanka.

Glossary

1) Dharma: righteousness
2) Rakshasa: demon